DK READERS

BEGINNING **1** TO READ

Feeding Time

Written by Lee Davis

DK

DK Publishing, Inc.

It is morning.
The sun is rising.
Animals that eat in the daytime
start to look for food.

A gorilla yawns in his nest.
He reaches out his hairy hand
to feel for a tasty plant.
He has breakfast in bed.

plant

A herd of elephants
is ready for breakfast, too.
The elephants wrap
their trunks around
clumps of grass.

They curl their trunks
to break off the grass
and put it in their mouths.

Another elephant snaps off
branches from a big tree.
He chews the bark
on each branch.

bark

A large elephant knows
there are some crunchy seed pods
in the tall trees.
He stretches his trunk
to reach them.

seed pods

Zebras reach down
to nibble the grass.

grass

They bite the grass
with their front teeth.

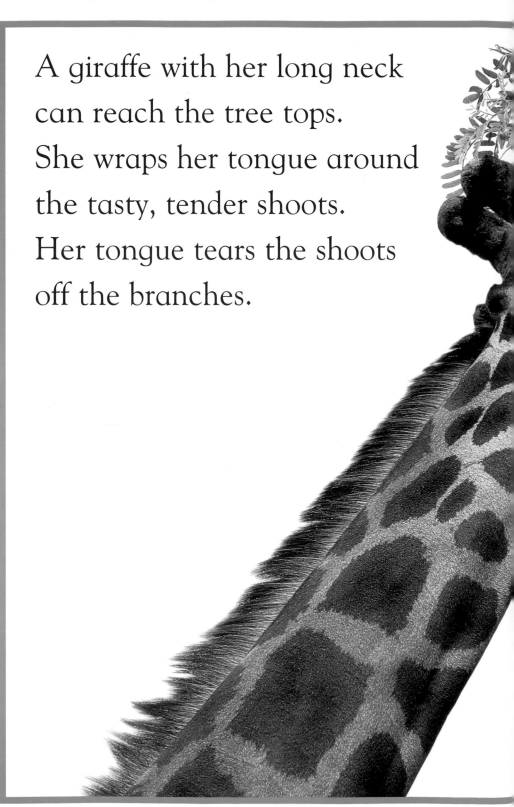

A giraffe with her long neck
can reach the tree tops.
She wraps her tongue around
the tasty, tender shoots.
Her tongue tears the shoots
off the branches.

shoots

banana

The elephants wander
through the forest.
They find some banana plants.
They shake the branches
to make the bananas fall off.

A rhino spends most of the day eating grass.

An oxpecker clings to the rhino.

The oxpecker eats ticks
and insects on the rhino's skin.
He pecks at them
with his pointed beak.

tick

A chimpanzee is looking
for termites to eat.
He digs with a stick
into a huge termite hill.
He makes a large hole
in the termite hill
and the termites spill out.

termites

Elephants need to eat salt.
They do not get enough salt
in their food.
So they dig up
clumps of salt to eat.

A herd of buffalo
moves to the river
for a drink.
Crocodiles watch and wait.
They are as still as rocks.

Slowly, a crocodile
swims closer.
Can he grab
a young buffalo
for his dinner?

Hippos spend the hot day
in the water.

In the evening, the air is cooler.
So they come out
to eat the short grass
on the river banks.

As the sun sets,
the elephants enjoy
a late evening snack.

DK READERS

Which animal enjoys breakfast in bed? Which ones eat all the time? Discover how African animals find their food.

DK READERS

Stunning photographs combine with lively illustrations and engaging, age-appropriate stories in DK READERS, a multilevel reading program guaranteed to capture children's interest while developing their reading skills and general knowledge.

LEARNING pre-level **1** TO READ	Learning to read	• High-frequency words • Picture word strips, picture glossary, and simple index • Labels to introduce and reinforce vocabulary • High level of adult participation helpful
BEGINNING **1** TO READ	Beginning to read	• Simple sentences and limited vocabulary • Picture glossary and simple index • Adult participation helpful
BEGINNING **2** TO READ ALONE	Beginning to read alone	• Longer sentences and increased vocabulary • Information boxes full of extra fun facts • Simple index • Occasional adult participation helpful
READING **3** ALONE	Reading alone	• More complex sentence structure • Information boxes and alphabetical glossary • Comprehensive index
PROFICIENT **4** READERS	Proficient readers	• Rich vocabulary and challenging sentence structure • Additional information and alphabetical glossary • Comprehensive index

With DK READERS, children will learn to read—then read to learn!

DK

Discover more
www.dk.com

$3.99 USA
$4.99 Canada

DK READERS

My name is

MYLeS

I have read this book

Date

3/19/12

Picture word list

plant

page 7

shoots

page 17

bark

page 10

banana

page 19

seed pods

page 12

tick

page 21

grass

page 14

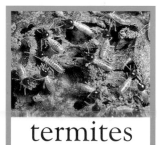

termites

page 22

Maybe some more fruit
and then a long, cool drink!